D1283747

APPETIZERS

BRIMAR

Editor Angela Rahaniotis
Graphic Design Zapp
Photography Marc Bruneau
Food Preparation / Stylist Josée Robitaille
Assistant Stylist Marc Maula
Tableware courtesy of Stokes
                         Danesco Inc.
                         Ceramistes Goyer Bonneau

© 1995 Brimar Publishing Inc.
338 Saint Antoine St. East
Montreal, Canada H2Y 1A3
Tel.: (514) 954-1441
Fax: (514) 954-5086

ISBN 2-89433-149-5
Printed in Canada

APPETIZERS

Appetizers set the mood for everything
that follows, and add a note of refinement
to even the simplest meal.

But appetizers don't necessarily have
to be complicated and time-consuming.
The appetizers in this cookbook have been
carefully selected to provide you with a range
of easy and tasty starter courses and cocktail
snacks ranging from the elegantly simple
to the impressively grand.

Each recipe is accompanied by
easy-to-follow instructions and a color
photograph to guide you in the all-important
art of presentation and visual appeal.

In fact, with this cookbook, you will discover
just how easy it is to turn out the perfect
appetizer for any occasion.

Dough for Tartlets

3¾ cups	sifted all-purpose flour	925 mL
1½ tsp	salt	7 mL
½ lb	unsalted butter, chilled	225 g
¾ cup	cold water	175 mL

1 Sift flour and salt into food processor.

2 Cut butter into pieces and distribute over flour. Blend until mixture resembles cornmeal.

3 Add water, a little at a time, blending between additions until dough forms ball. If necessary, add more water to obtain desired consistency.

4 Remove dough from food processor and shape into smooth ball. Wrap in clean cloth and refrigerate 2 hours.

5 Bring dough to room temperature before using.

How to Precook Tartlets

•

Tartlet molds come in a variety of shapes
but are generally of similar size.

•

Bring dough to room temperature before using.

•

Shape dough into cylinder and cut into pieces about 2 in (5 cm) wide.
Roll out each piece of dough on floured surface into circle
about ⅛ in (3 mm) thick.

•

Line tartlet molds, pressing dough snug against bottom and sides.
Line dough with waxed paper and fill with baking weights
or dried beans.

•

Arrange molds on cookie sheet and bake 10 minutes
in oven preheated at 400°F (200°C).

•

Remove waxed paper and baking weights from tartlets
and let cool before filling.

How to Deep-Fry Vegetables

•

Choose vegetables in season. Some good choices are: zucchini, carrots, celery, mushrooms, onions, bell peppers, cauliflower and broccoli.

•

Cut vegetables into uniform pieces and place in bowl. Season with olive oil, lemon juice, fresh herbs in season and chopped garlic. If desired, add a few drops of hot pepper sauce.

•

Season with salt and pepper. Mix well and marinate vegetables 10 minutes.

•

Coat vegetables in batter, such as Beer Batter for Deep-Frying Vegetables (see page 7).

•

Fry in plenty of hot peanut oil. When vegetables turn golden brown, remove and let drain on paper towels.

•

Serve with lemon juice or a variety of dipping sauces.

Beer Batter for Deep-Frying Vegetables

1 cup	all-purpose flour	250 mL
3 tbsp	olive oil	45 mL
1 cup	beer, at room temperature	250 mL
3	eggs, separated	3
	salt	

1 Place flour in bowl. Add oil, salt and beer. Incorporate until smooth using whisk.

2 Whisk in egg yolks and let batter stand 30 minutes at room temperature.

3 Beat egg whites until soft peaks form; fold into batter.

4 Use to deep-fry your choice of vegetables. Serve with a dipping sauce.

Canapés with Tuna and Egg
(6 to 8 servings)

3	hard-boiled eggs, mashed	3
5 oz	can tuna, drained	142 g
1 tbsp	chopped pimiento pepper	15 mL
1	yellow bell pepper, chopped	1
2 tbsp	sour cream	30 mL
2 tbsp	capers	30 mL
	salt and freshly ground pepper	
	few drops of Tabasco sauce	
	few drops of lemon juice	

1 Place mashed eggs, tuna and remaining ingredients in bowl. Mix together until well combined. Add more sour cream to taste.

2 Spread on a variety of crackers and toasted bread.

Figs and Prosciutto
(4 servings)

4	fresh ripe figs, halved	4
8	asparagus stalks, cooked	8
8	slices prosciutto	8
½ cup	sour cream	125 mL
1 tbsp	chopped capers	15 mL
1	shallot, peeled and chopped	1
	salt and freshly ground pepper	
	pinch of paprika	
	lemon juice	

1 Wrap each fig half and one asparagus stalk together in slice of prosciutto. Arrange on serving platter.

2 Mix sour cream with remaining ingredients. Correct seasoning and place in small serving bowl.

3 Accompany with lemon wedges, if desired.

* See photograph on cover.

Steamed Mussels with Mustard Cream
(6 servings)

6½ lb	fresh mussels, bearded and scrubbed	3 kg
½ cup	dry white wine	125 mL
2	dry shallots, peeled and sliced	2
½ cup	water	125 mL
½ cup	heavy cream	125 mL
1 tbsp	Dijon mustard	15 mL
	lemon juice to taste	
	freshly ground pepper	
	lettuce leaves	
	chopped fresh parsley	
	lemon wedges (optional)	

1 Place mussels in large pot. Add wine, shallots and water. Cover and bring to boil. Cook mussels over low heat until shells open, about 5 minutes. Stir once during cooking.

2 Remove mussels from pot, discarding any unopened shells. Remove mussels from opened shells and place in bowl.

3 Mix cream with mustard and lemon juice; season well. Pour over mussels, mix well and serve on lettuce leaves. Garnish with fresh parsley. Serve with lemon wedges, if desired.

Cabbage Leaf Bundles
(6 to 8 servings)

16	small cabbage leaves	16
2 tbsp	olive oil	30 mL
2	onions, peeled and thinly sliced	2
1	red bell pepper, thinly sliced	1
2	garlic cloves, peeled and sliced	2
1 ½ cups	cooked white rice	375 mL
½ cup	pitted black olives, halved	125 mL
1 tbsp	chopped fresh basil	15 mL
½ cup	cottage cheese	125 mL
	salt and pepper	
	cayenne pepper to taste	
	French vinaigrette	
	chives	

1 Blanch cabbage leaves 4 minutes in salted, boiling water. Drain well and set aside on paper towels.

2 Heat oil in frying pan over medium heat. Add onions and cook 6 minutes. Stir in bell pepper and garlic; season well. Continue cooking 7 minutes.

3 Transfer mixture to bowl. Incorporate rice, olives, basil and cheese. Season generously with salt, pepper and cayenne pepper.

4 Place small amount of stuffing on each cabbage leaf. Fold and wrap into tight bundle. Tie with chives.

5 Arrange in single layer on serving platter. Serve with French vinaigrette.

Blanch cabbage leaves 4 minutes in salted, boiling water. Drain well and set aside on paper towels.

Heat oil in frying pan over medium heat. Add onions and cook 6 minutes. Stir in bell pepper and garlic; season well. Continue cooking 7 minutes.

Transfer mixture to bowl. Incorporate rice, olives, basil and cheese. Season generously with salt, pepper and cayenne pepper.

Place small amount of stuffing on each cabbage leaf.

Fold and wrap into tight bundle. Tie with chives.

Marinated Strip Loin
(4 to 6 servings)

3 tbsp	olive oil	45 mL
2	strip loin steaks, ¾ in (2 cm) thick	2
2	dry shallots, peeled and thinly sliced	2
1 tbsp	Worcestershire sauce	15 mL
2 tbsp	balsamic vinegar	30 mL
2 tbsp	chopped fresh basil	30 mL
½	jalapeño pepper, seeded and chopped	½
	salt and pepper	

1 Heat 1 tbsp (15 mL) oil in frying pan over medium heat. When very hot, add steaks and cook 3 minutes on one side. Turn meat over, season well and continue cooking 3 minutes. Season well.

2 Remove steaks from pan and set aside on cutting board. Mix remaining ingredients together in small bowl.

3 Slice steaks thinly and arrange on serving platter. Pour sauce over meat and marinate 1 hour in refrigerator.

4 Season well and serve on lettuce leaves.

Cool Cheesy Cucumber Slices
(6 servings)

2 - 3	cucumbers	2 - 3
½	lemon	½
1	red bell pepper	1
6 oz	soft cream cheese	175 g
1 tbsp	sour cream	15 mL
1 tbsp	chopped fresh basil	15 mL
1 tbsp	chopped fresh chives	15 mL
2	blanched garlic cloves, puréed	2
	salt and pepper	
	pinch of paprika	

1 Slice cucumbers in half, lengthwise. Peel and remove seeds using apple corer. Hollow out shells to make cavity for filling. Rub all sides of cucumbers with lemon. Season cavities with salt and pepper; set aside.

2 Cut bell pepper in half and remove seeds. Oil skin and place cut-side-down on cookie sheet; broil 6 minutes in oven. Remove from oven and let cool. Peel off skin and chop pepper finely; place in large bowl.

3 Add cream cheese, sour cream, fresh herbs and garlic to bowl. Mix well. Season with salt, pepper and paprika.

4 Fill cucumber cavities with mixture. Cover tightly with plastic wrap and refrigerate 2 hours.

5 Slice and serve on lettuce leaves.

Marinated Eggplant Spread
(6 to 10 servings)

6	garlic cloves	6
3	fresh parsley sprigs	3
1	fresh thyme sprig	1
1	jalapeño pepper, halved and seeded	1
12	black peppercorns	12
2 cups	white vinegar	500 mL
2 tbsp	sugar	30 mL
2	medium eggplants, sliced ¼ in (5 mm) thick	2
	chopped zest of 1 lemon	
	pickling spices to taste	
	salt and freshly ground pepper	

1 Place garlic, fresh herbs, jalapeño pepper, peppercorns, lemon zest and pickling spices in piece of cheesecloth. Secure with string and place in saucepan.

2 Add vinegar, sugar and salt to saucepan. Cook 6 minutes over medium heat.

3 Arrange eggplant slices in single layer in roasting pan. Pour vinegar dressing over eggplant. Season well with pepper. Cover with plastic wrap and marinate in refrigerator 12 hours.

4 Remove eggplant slices and pat dry with paper towels. Purée and correct seasoning. Serve as dip for toast, crackers and tortilla chips.

Zesty Bell Pepper-Tomato Chip Dip
(6 to 10 servings)

3 tbsp	olive oil	45 mL
2	onions, peeled and thinly sliced	2
5	garlic cloves, peeled, crushed and chopped	5
4	red bell peppers, thinly sliced	4
4	tomatoes, peeled, seeded and chopped	4
	salt and freshly ground pepper	
	tortilla chips	

1 Heat oil in sauté pan over medium heat. Add onions, season and cook 10 minutes over low heat. Stir occasionally.

2 Add garlic and bell peppers. Season, cover and continue cooking 15 minutes.

3 Stir in tomatoes and cook 25 minutes. Do not cover. Stir occasionally.

4 Serve cold with tortillas chips.

Roasted Goat Cheese
(6 to 8 servings)

3 tbsp	finely chopped almonds	45 mL
1 tbsp	white breadcrumbs	15 mL
1 lb	medium-soft goat cheese	450 g
	pinch of cayenne pepper	
	olive oil	

Preheat oven to 400°F (200°C).

1 Slice cheese into 6 or 8 rounds.

2 Mix almonds with breadcrumbs and cayenne pepper.

3 Roll cheese in mixture until well coated; roll briefly in olive oil.

4 Place on cookie sheet and roast in oven. Rotate cheese during roasting. Remove from oven when cheese is browned evenly.

5 Place on platter and serve warm.

Shrimp à la Catalan
(4 to 6 servings)

2 tbsp	olive oil	30 mL
2	dry shallots, peeled and finely chopped	2
3	garlic cloves, peeled, crushed and chopped	3
3	tomatoes, peeled, seeded and chopped	3
½ cup	dry white wine	125 mL
1 tbsp	chopped fresh basil	15 mL
½	roasted red bell pepper, peeled and diced	½
1 lb	large shrimp, cooked, peeled and deveined	450 g
	pinch of saffron	
	salt and pepper	

1 Heat oil in frying pan over medium heat. Add shallots and garlic; cook 2 minutes. Add tomatoes, wine and saffron; season well. Cook 6 minutes over high heat.

2 Add basil and diced bell pepper; correct seasoning.

3 Place shrimp in sauce and simmer 2 to 3 minutes. Serve.

Avocado-Stuffed Cherry Tomatoes
(4 to 6 servings)

24	large cherry tomatoes	24
1	large ripe avocado	1
1 tsp	curry powder	5 mL
2 tbsp	grated onion	30 mL
	salt and freshly ground pepper	
	extra virgin olive oil	
	lemon juice	
	cayenne pepper to taste	
	sour cream	

1 Cut off top from tomatoes and remove most of pulp. Season cavities generously and add few drops of olive oil.

2 Cut avocado in half lengthwise. Twist halves apart and remove pit. Peel and mash flesh. Place in bowl.

3 Add curry powder, onion and lemon juice. Season generously with salt, pepper and cayenne pepper. Mix until well combined.

4 Stuff tomato shells and chill 30 minutes before serving. Serve with a dollop of sour cream.

Sicilian Canapés
(6 servings)

2	bell peppers	2
3 tbsp	olive oil	45 mL
1	large garlic clove, peeled	1
1	large eggplant, sliced ⅓ in (8 mm) thick	1
1 cup	grated Emmenthal cheese	250 mL
	salt and pepper	
	lemon juice to taste	
	cayenne pepper to taste	
	slices of toasted Italian bread	

1 Cut bell peppers in half and remove seeds. Oil skin and place cut-side-down on cookie sheet; broil 6 minutes in oven. Remove from oven and let cool. Peel off skin, slice peppers and set aside.

2 Heat oil in large frying pan over high heat. Add garlic clove and cook 1 to 2 minutes. Discard garlic.

3 Add half of eggplant slices to hot oil. Season well and cook 3 minutes on each side. Remove slices and set aside. Add remaining eggplant to pan and repeat process.

4 Return first batch of eggplant to hot pan. Add bell peppers and lemon juice. Season with cayenne pepper. Simmer for 1 to 2 minutes.

5 Top toasted bread with eggplant mixture. Arrange on cookie sheet, season well and cover with cheese.

6 Broil 3 minutes, cut in triangles or rectangles and serve.

Veal and Pork Pâté
(12 to 18 servings)

¼ lb	pork liver, cleaned	125 g
3 tbsp	cognac	45 mL
2¼ lb	boneless veal shoulder	1 kg
¼ lb	lean ground pork	125 g
1½ tsp (*each*)	salt, black pepper	7 mL
2	dry shallots, peeled and chopped	2
2	garlic cloves, peeled, crushed and chopped	2
2 tbsp	chopped fresh parsley	30 mL
½ tsp	thyme	2 mL
1 tbsp	green peppercorns, mashed	15 mL
1	egg	1
3 tbsp	heavy cream	45 mL
½ lb	pork fat, cut in wide strips	225 g
2	bay leaves	2

1 Place pork liver in bowl and pour in cognac. Marinate 1 hour in refrigerator.

2 Preheat oven to 325°F (160°C). Cut one quarter of veal shoulder into strips and set aside. Grind remaining veal shoulder and pork liver into clean bowl. Add ground pork and mix well. Add remaining ingredients, except reserved veal shoulder, strips of fat and bay leaves. Mix until well combined.

3 Test seasoning by frying small patty of mixture in hot oil. Taste and season accordingly.

4 Line pâté mold with strips of fat so that ends drape over sides. Pack half of meat mixture into mold.

Add even layer of veal shoulder strips; pack in remaining meat mixture. Cover with ends of fat and top with bay leaves. Cover mold.

5 Place mold in roasting pan and add 1 in (2.5 cm) of hot water in pan. Bake 1 hour. Reduce oven heat to 300°F (150°C). Continue cooking 1½ to 2 hours. The pâté's internal temperature when cooked should read 150°F (70°C).

6 Remove mold from oven and position a flat plate directly on top of pâté. Weigh down with heavy object for 3 hours. Remove weight and cover mold. Refrigerate 48 hours before serving.

Place ground meats in clean bowl. Add seasoning ingredients.

Test seasoning by frying small patty of mixture in hot oil.

Line pâté mold with strips of fat so that ends drape over sides of mold.

Pack half of meat mixture into mold. Add even layer of veal shoulder strips. Pack in remaining meat mixture.

Cover with overhanging fat and position bay leaves on top.

Celery Hearts – Parisian Style
(4 to 6 servings)

4 – 6	celery heart stalks*, washed	4 – 6
1 tsp	English mustard	5 mL
4	anchovy fillets, drained and finely chopped	4
2	garlic cloves, peeled and sliced	2
3 tbsp	tarragon wine vinegar	45 mL
½ cup	olive oil	125 mL
	salt and freshly ground pepper	
	pinch of paprika	
	juice of 1½ lemons	

1 Place celery hearts in salted, boiling water and cook 10 minutes over medium heat. Drain well and pat dry with paper towels. Place celery hearts in deep platter.

2 Mix remaining ingredients together in small bowl. Correct seasoning and pour dressing over celery.

3 Refrigerate 1 to 2 hours. Serve with fresh herbs in season, if desired.

* Choose the celery heart consisting of 3 or 4 ribs at the center of a regular celery stalk.

Chicken and Mushroom Tartlets
(4 to 6 servings)

6	tartlets, precooked	6
3 tbsp	butter	45 mL
2	dry shallots, peeled and chopped	2
2	green onions, chopped	2
½ lb	fresh mushrooms, cleaned and minced	225 g
1 cup	diced cooked chicken	250 mL
1 tsp	curry powder	5 mL
1½ cups	Basic White Sauce, heated (see page 94)	375 mL
1 cup	grated Gruyère cheese	250 mL
	salt and pepper	
	pinch of paprika	

Preheat oven to 400°F (200°C).

1 Place shells on cookie sheet. Cook 8 minutes in oven to brown lightly. Set aside.

2 Heat butter in frying pan over medium heat. Add shallots, green onions and mushrooms; season well. Cook 4 minutes over high heat.

3 Add chicken, curry powder and white sauce. Season, add paprika and mix well. Cook 2 minutes over low heat.

4 Fill tartlets with mixture and top with cheese. Change oven setting to broil and brown 3 minutes. Serve warm.

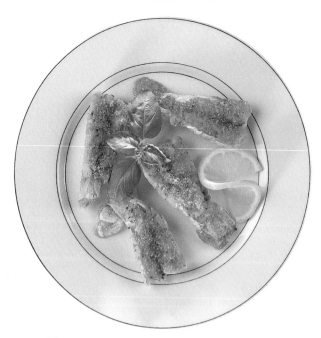

Broiled Scampi with Garlic Butter
(4 servings)

16	scampi, peeled, deveined and butterflied	16
½ lb	softened unsalted butter	225 g
2	large garlic cloves, peeled, crushed and chopped	2
2 tbsp	chopped fresh parsley	30 mL
1 tbsp	chopped fresh basil	15 mL
½ cup	white breadcrumbs	125 mL
	salt and freshly ground pepper	
	few drops of Tabasco sauce	
	lemon juice	

1 Arrange scampi in single layer in large baking tray. Set aside.

2 Mix remaining ingredients together, except breadcrumbs, until well incorporated. Spread garlic butter over scampi.

3 Sprinkle with breadcrumbs and broil 5 minutes. Serve with lemon slices, if desired.

Sauté of Scampi with Brandy
(4 servings)

3 tbsp	butter	45 mL
1	carrot, pared and minced	1
2	dry shallots, peeled and chopped	2
16	scampi, peeled and deveined	16
3 tbsp	brandy	45 mL
1 cup	dry white wine	250 mL
½ cup	clam juice	125 mL
1 tsp	cornstarch	5 mL
3 tbsp	cold water	45 mL
1 tbsp	chopped fresh parsley	15 mL
	salt and freshly ground pepper	

1 Heat butter in sauté pan over medium heat. Add carrot, shallots and scampi; season well. Cook 3 minutes. Pour in brandy and cook 1 minute. Remove scampi and set aside.

2 Add wine to pan and cook 2 minutes over high heat. Stir in clam juice and continue cooking 1 to 2 minutes.

3 Dilute cornstarch in cold water. Stir into sauce and cook 1 minute over low heat.

4 Return scampi to pan, mix and add parsley. Correct seasoning and simmer 1 minute before serving. Accompany with spinach, if desired.

Cheesy Eggplant-Bacon Sandwiches
(4 to 6 servings)

1	medium eggplant	1
¼ cup	olive oil	50 mL
¼ cup	grated Parmesan cheese	50 mL
1 cup	grated mozzarella cheese	250 mL
½ cup	crisp cooked chopped bacon	125 mL
2	eggs, beaten	2
1 cup	white breadcrumbs	250 mL
	salt and freshly ground pepper	
	flour	

1 Slice eggplant crosswise, ¼ in (5 mm) thick. Arrange eggplant slices in single layer in roasting pan and sprinkle generously with salt. Let stand 1 hour at room temperature. Drain off excess liquid and rinse salt from eggplant slices. Pat dry with paper towels.

2 Heat half of oil in frying pan over high heat. Add eggplant slices and cook 4 minutes on each side. Do not overcook.

3 Arrange half of eggplant slices on cookie sheet. Cover each with grated cheeses, season well and top with bacon. Position remaining eggplant slices to make sandwiches and press down with metal spatula. Refrigerate 30 minutes.

4 Dredge eggplant sandwiches in flour. Dip in beaten eggs and coat thoroughly in breadcrumbs.

5 Heat remaining oil in frying pan over medium heat. Add eggplant sandwiches and brown 6 minutes on each side. Slice and serve.

French Cheese Party Squares
(6 to 10 servings)

9	slices day old French bread	9
3	large eggs, separated	3
½ cup	milk	125 mL
¾ cup	light cream	175 mL
¾ cup	diced Gruyère cheese	175 mL
½ cup	diced cheddar cheese	125 mL
2 tbsp	chopped fresh basil	30 mL
	salt and freshly ground pepper	
	pinch of paprika	

Preheat oven to 350°F (180°C).

1 Remove crust from bread and discard. Dice bread and set aside.

2 Place egg yolks in bowl with milk and cream. Beat well. Season with salt, pepper and paprika. Add bread, both cheeses and basil. Mix well.

3 Place egg whites in separate bowl and beat until stiff. Carefully fold into bread mixture. Pour batter into buttered square baking dish.

4 Bake 25 to 30 minutes or until done. Remove from oven and let cool slightly. Cut into squares and serve.

Coquille of Mushroom and Spinach
(4 servings)

1 lb	fresh mushrooms, cleaned	450 g
2 tbsp	olive oil	30 mL
2	dry shallots, peeled and chopped	2
1 cup	heavy cream	250 mL
2	bunches fresh spinach, cooked	2
½ cup	white breadcrumbs	125 mL
	salt and pepper	

1 Remove stems from mushrooms and chop. Dice caps.

2 Heat oil in frying pan over medium heat. Add diced mushroom caps and season well. Cook 6 minutes over high heat to evaporate moisture.

3 Add remaining chopped mushrooms and shallots to pan. Continue cooking 5 minutes. Pour in cream and cook 4 minutes over high heat.

4 Chop spinach and line bottoms of ovenproof coquille dishes. Top with mushroom mixture and sprinkle with breadcrumbs. Broil 2 minutes and serve.

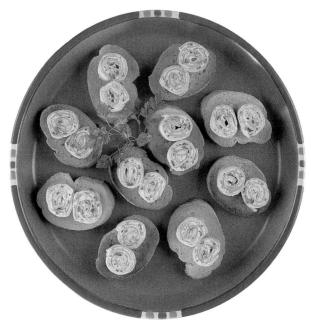

Sun-Dried Tomato Ham Rolls

(4 to 6 servings)

⅓ cup	chopped pimiento pepper	75 mL
1 tbsp	chopped fresh parsley	15 mL
⅓ cup	soft cream cheese	75 mL
2 tbsp	finely chopped sun-dried tomatoes	30 mL
12	thin slices cooked ham	12
	freshly ground pepper	
	cayenne pepper to taste	
	lemon juice	

1 Place all ingredients, except ham, in bowl. Mix well and correct seasoning according to taste.

2 Lay ham slices flat on work surface. Spread cheese mixture on each slice and roll up into cylindrical shape.

3 Place ham rolls, seam-side-down, on large dinner plate. Position second plate on top of ham and refrigerate 1 hour.

4 Cut ham rolls in half and serve.

Lamb and Mushroom on Skewers
(4 servings)

½ lb	lamb kidney, cleaned and trimmed of fat	225 g
½ lb	small mushroom caps, cleaned	225 g
	olive oil	
	chopped fresh rosemary	
	lemon juice	
	salt and freshly ground pepper	
	pinch of paprika	

Preheat oven to 375°F (190°C)

1 Cut kidney into ¾ in (2 cm) pieces. Thread, alternating with mushroom caps, on short wooden skewers.

2 Mix olive oil and fresh rosemary together. Baste skewers and sprinkle with lemon juice. Season with salt, pepper and paprika.

3 Change oven setting to broil. Cook skewers 1 to 2 minutes on each side about 6 in (15 cm) from top element. Baste during cooking.

4 Season and serve hot.

Mushroom Caps Stuffed with Snails
(4 to 6 servings)

2 tbsp	olive oil	30 mL
16 – 24	large mushrooms caps, cleaned	16 – 24
16 – 24	snails, washed and drained well	16 – 24
⅓ lb	softened garlic butter (see page 94)	150 g
	freshly ground pepper	

1 Heat oil in frying pan over medium heat. Add mushrooms and cook 7 minutes over high heat to evaporate water content. Season with pepper and remove mushrooms from pan. Let cool.

2 Place one snail in each mushroom cap. Spread garlic butter over snail to cover.

3 Arrange stuffed mushrooms on cookie sheet. Broil 5 minutes in oven. Serve.

Fish Balls
(6 to 8 servings)

2 tbsp	olive oil	30 mL
1	onion, peeled and chopped	1
3	small sole fillets, poached	3
2	garlic cloves, peeled, crushed and chopped	2
2	boiled potatoes, mashed	2
1 tbsp	chopped fresh ginger	15 mL
2 tbsp	chopped pimiento pepper	30 mL
2	eggs, beaten	2
1 cup	breadcrumbs	250 mL
	salt and pepper	
	flour	
	oil for deep-frying	

1 Heat olive oil in frying pan over medium heat. Add onion and cook 3 minutes over low heat. Add fish and garlic. Season and mix well. Cook 4 minutes over medium heat.

2 Stir in potatoes, ginger and pimiento pepper. Blend well. Cook 3 minutes over high heat.

3 Remove pan from heat and let mixture cool. Shape into small balls and dredge in flour.

4 Dip in beaten eggs and roll in breadcrumbs. Deep-fry in hot oil until golden brown; about 2 minutes. Serve with your favorite spicy sauce.

Eggplant Fritters
(6 to 12 servings)

3	medium eggplants	3
1 cup	all-purpose flour	250 mL
2 tbsp	olive oil	30 mL
¾ cup	warm water	175 mL
1	large egg white, beaten stiff	1
	salt and freshly ground pepper	
	oil for deep-frying	

1 Cut eggplants into round slices ¼-in (5-mm) thick. Arrange in single layer in roasting pan and sprinkle generously with salt. Let stand 3 hours at room temperature. Drain off excess liquid and rinse salt from eggplant slices. Pat dry with paper towels.

2 Sift flour with ½ tsp (2 mL) salt into bowl. Add oil and water; blend together. Cover batter and refrigerate 1 hour before using.

3 Fold beaten egg white into batter. Dip eggplant slices in batter and deep-fry in hot oil until golden brown. Drain on paper towels before serving. Season generously.

Pumpernickel Canapés
(4 servings)

2 tbsp	butter	30 mL
1 tsp	horseradish	5 mL
1 tsp	Dijon mustard	5 mL
4	large slices pumpernickel bread	4
4	slices roast beef, folded in half	4
4	slices pastrami, folded in half	4
2	hard-boiled eggs, sliced	2
	freshly ground pepper	

1 Mix butter with horseradish and mustard. Spread on one side of bread and arrange on serving platter.

2 Cover each slice of bread with folded slice of roast beef on one half, and folded slice of pastrami on the other. Season with pepper.

3 Decorate canapés with hard-boiled egg slices. Accompany with assorted pickles.

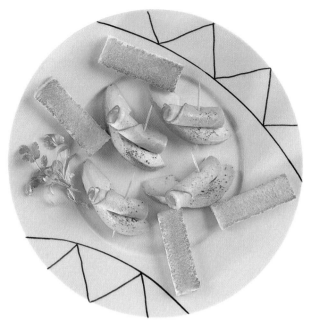

Avocado Virginia
(4 servings)

1	large ripe avocado	1
¼ cup	mustard vinaigrette	50 mL
4	slices Virginia ham, rolled	4
	lemon juice	
	freshly ground pepper	

1 Cut avocado in half, lengthwise. Twist halves apart and remove pit. Cut into wedges and place on platter.

2 Pour vinaigrette over avocado. Marinate 3 to 4 minutes.

3 Arrange avocado wedges decoratively on small plates. Accompany each serving with ham roll.

4 Sprinkle with lemon juice and season with pepper.

Bay Scallops with Pernod
(4 to 6 servings)

3 tbsp	butter	45 mL
¾ lb	bay scallops, cleaned	350 g
24	fresh mushrooms, cleaned and quartered	24
2	dry shallots, peeled and chopped	2
1 tbsp	chopped fresh parsley	15 mL
1 tsp	chopped fresh tarragon	5 mL
3 tbsp	Pernod	45 mL
¾ cup	heavy cream	175 mL
1 cup	grated Gruyère cheese	250 mL
	pinch of celery seeds	
	salt and freshly ground pepper	
	cayenne pepper to taste	

1 Heat half of butter in frying pan over medium heat. Add scallops and cook 1 minute over high heat. Transfer scallops to sieve and set over bowl to collect juices.

2 Add remaining butter to hot pan. When melted, add mushrooms and shallots. Sprinkle in fresh herbs, celery seeds and season well. Cook 4 minutes over high heat.

3 Add juices from scallops and continue cooking 2 minutes. Add Pernod and cook 1 minute. Pour in cream, correct seasoning and mix well. Cook 3 minutes over high heat.

4 When sauce thickens, add scallops and mix well. Spoon into ovenproof coquille dishes and top with cheese.

5 Broil 3 minutes until golden brown. Serve.

Escargots with Shallot Butter
(4 servings)

½ lb	softened unsalted butter	225 g
3	dry shallots, peeled and finely chopped	3
4	garlic cloves, peeled, crushed and finely chopped	4
3 tbsp	chopped fresh parsley	45 mL
24	snail shells	24
24	canned snails, rinsed and dried	24
	salt and freshly ground pepper	
	cayenne pepper to taste	
	lemon juice	

Preheat oven to 400°F (200°C).

1 Place butter, shallots, garlic, parsley and all seasonings in bowl. Using wooden spoon, blend to obtain smooth consistency.

2 Place small amount of butter in each snail shell. Add snail and cover with more butter. Arrange in escargot dishes.

3 Place in oven and cook 6 minutes. Be careful not to burn butter. Serve with French baguette.

Tasty Chinese Rolls
(6 to 8 servings)

½	head cabbage, shredded	½
¼ lb	barbecued pork, shredded	125 g
¼ lb	shrimp, cooked, peeled, deveined and thinly sliced	125 g
2 cups	bean sprouts	500 mL
½ tsp	Chinese seasoning	2 mL
2 tbsp	soy sauce	30 mL
3 tbsp	sugar	45 mL
1½ tsp	salt	7 mL
1	egg	1
3 tbsp	flour	45 mL
1	bamboo shoot, thinly sliced	1
8	wonton wrappers	8
	few drops of sesame oil	
	freshly ground pepper	
	plum sauce	
	oil for deep-frying	

1 Blanch shredded cabbage in salted, boiling water for 2 minutes. Drain well and pat dry with paper towels.

2 Place cabbage in bowl. Add pork, shrimp, bean sprouts, Chinese seasoning, soy sauce, sugar and salt. Mix and stir in egg, then flour. Add bamboo shoot and few drops of sesame oil. Season with pepper and mix well.

3 Lay wonton wrappers flat on work surface. Moisten edges with water and spread stuffing along middle of wrapper. Roll up wrapper to cover stuffing and fold in sides to close ends. Finish rolling wrapper and seal seam with a little water.

4 Deep-fry in hot oil until golden brown. Serve with plum sauce.

Lay wonton wrappers flat on work surface. Moisten edges with water.

Spread stuffing along middle of wrapper.

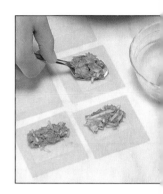

Roll up wrapper to cover stuffing and fold in sides to close ends.

Finish rolling wrapper and seal seam with a little water.

Fillets of Sole Surprise
(4 servings)

4	large tomatoes	4
2 cups	water	500 mL
1 cup	dry white wine	250 mL
1	onion, peeled and sliced	1
⅓	celery rib, sliced	⅓
2	fresh parsley sprigs	2
4	thin sole fillets	4
4 tbsp	caviar	60 mL
4 tbsp	Egg Dressing (see page 95)	60 mL
	salt and freshly ground pepper	
	few drops of olive oil	
	lemon slices	

1 Slice top off tomatoes and remove most of pulp with spoon. Season cavities well and add few drops of oil. Set tomatoes aside.

2 Place water, wine, onion, celery and parsley in saucepan. Season well and bring to boil.

3 Roll sole fillets and secure with string. Poach 2 minutes in hot liquid. Remove and let cool.

4 Remove string and place rolled fillets in tomato cavities. Spoon caviar into hole of sole fillet roll and top with egg dressing. Garnish with lemon and serve.

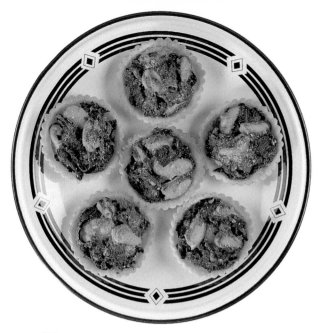

Tartlets with Mussels and Spinach
(4 to 6 servings)

6	tartlets, precooked	6
3 tbsp	butter	45 mL
3	dry shallots, peeled and coarsely chopped	3
1	large garlic clove, peeled, crushed and chopped	1
1 tbsp	chopped fresh chervil	15 mL
1 tbsp	chopped fresh parsley	15 mL
½ cup	packed fresh spinach, well cleaned	125 mL
16 – 24	cooked mussels	16 – 24
½ cup	white breadcrumbs	125 mL
	salt and freshly ground pepper	
	lemon juice to taste	

Preheat oven to 400°F (200°C).

1 Place tartlet shells on cookie sheet.Cook 8 minutes in oven to brown lightly. Set aside.

2 Heat butter in frying pan over medium heat. Add shallots, garlic, herbs and spinach. Season well and cook 6 minutes over high heat.

3 Add mussels and continue cooking 1 minute. Add lemon juice to taste. Fill tartlets with mixture and sprinkle with breadcrumbs.

4 Change oven setting to broil and brown 3 minutes. Serve warm.

Fried Marinated Scallops
(4 to 8 servings)

1 lb	fresh scallops, washed	450 g
2	garlic cloves, peeled and sliced	2
2 tbsp	teriyaki sauce	30 mL
1 tbsp	sesame oil	15 mL
½ cup	flour	125 mL
2	eggs, beaten	2
¾ cup	breadcrumbs	175 mL
	juice of 1½ lemons	
	crushed chilies	
	pepper	
	oil for deep-frying	

1 Place scallops in large bowl. Add garlic, teriyaki sauce, sesame oil and lemon juice. Stir in crushed chilies and season well with pepper. Cover with plastic wrap and chill 1 hour.

2 Drain scallops well and dredge in flour. Dip in beaten eggs and roll in breadcrumbs.

3 Deep-fry in hot oil 2 to 3 minutes. Drain on paper towels and serve.

Snails in Puff Pastry
(4 servings)

2 tbsp	olive oil	30 mL
1	onion, peeled and finely chopped	1
2	garlic cloves, peeled, crushed and chopped	2
1 tbsp	chopped fresh basil	15 mL
1 tbsp	chopped fresh parsley	15 mL
3	tomatoes, peeled, seeded and chopped	3
2 tbsp	flour	30 mL
1 cup	dry white wine	250 mL
24	canned snails, rinsed and dried	24
4	small vol-au-vent pastry shells*	4
	salt and freshly ground pepper	
	cayenne pepper to taste	

1 Heat oil in sauté pan over medium heat. Add onion and garlic; cook 3 minutes.

2 Stir in seasonings and tomatoes. Cook 12 minutes over medium heat, stirring occasionally.

3 Sprinkle in flour and mix well. Cook 2 minutes. Pour in wine, mix and cook 5 minutes.

4 Add snails and simmer 4 minutes or until heated through.

5 Place warm vol-au-vent pastry shells on plate. Fill with snail mixture and spoon some of stuffing on plate. Serve.

* Use good quality frozen vol-au-vent shells. Follow directions on package and bake in oven before filling.

Tomatoes Stuffed with Smoked Salmon
(4 servings)

4	tomatoes	4
1 tbsp	butter	15 mL
3	dry shallots, peeled and chopped	3
3 oz	smoked salmon, diced	90 g
1 tbsp	chopped fresh basil	15 mL
3 tbsp	sour cream	45 mL
	salt and freshly ground pepper	
	few drops of olive oil	
	lemon juice	

1 Slice top off tomatoes and re- move most of pulp with spoon. Season cavities well and add few drops of oil. Set tomatoes aside.

2 Heat butter in frying pan over medium heat. Add shallots and cook 2 minutes over low heat.

3 Add smoked salmon, season with pepper and cook 1 minute. Remove salmon from pan and set aside.

4 Add basil and sour cream to hot pan. Mix well and add lemon juice to taste. Remove pan from heat and stir in salmon.

5 Fill tomatoes with salmon mix- ture and serve cold.

Lobster Cocktail
(4 servings)

2 lb	lobster, boiled and meat removed	900 g
2	hard-boiled eggs, diced	2
¼ cup	mayonnaise	50 mL
2 tbsp	chili sauce	30 mL
2 tbsp	catsup	30 mL
I tsp	horseradish	5 mL
I tsp	Dijon mustard	5 mL
	lemon juice	
	lettuce leaves	
	salt and freshly ground pepper	
	few drops of Tabasco sauce	
	lemon wedges	

1 Place lobster meat and diced eggs in bowl. Add lemon juice to taste and season well; mix.

2 Place mayonnaise, chili sauce, catsup, horseradish and mustard in small bowl. Mix together. Add lemon juice and season well. Add few drops of Tabasco sauce.

3 Add cocktail sauce to lobster mixture. Mix and arrange on plates lined with lettuce. Accompany with lemon wedges.

Meatballs with Hot Salsa
(6 to 8 servings)

HOT SALSA:

2 cups	diced fresh tomatoes	500 mL
2	blanched garlic cloves, puréed	2
2 tbsp	chopped fresh cilantro	30 mL
1	serrano chili pepper, finely chopped	1
½	small red onion, chopped	½
	salt and pepper	

1 Mix all ingredients together and refrigerate 1 hour before serving.

MEATBALLS:

1½ lb	lean ground beef	700 g
1	onion, peeled, chopped and cooked	1
3	blanched garlic cloves, puréed	3
¼ cup	grated Parmesan cheese	50 mL
1 tbsp	Worcestershire sauce	15 mL
1	egg	1
2 tbsp	olive oil	30 mL
	pinch of ground clove	
	salt and freshly ground pepper	
	crushed chilies to taste	
	oil for frying	

1 Place all ingredients in food processor. Blend together until well combined.

2 Grease hands with oil and shape meat into small meatballs.

3 Fry meatballs in hot oil over medium heat in several batches. Drain on paper towels. Serve with hot salsa.

Smoked Sausage Brochettes
(4 servings)

2	smoked sausages, sliced on the bias ¼ in (5 mm) thick	2
1	green bell pepper, cut in big pieces	1
12	cubes Gruyère cheese	12
12	cherry tomatoes, cored	12
3 tbsp	olive oil	45 mL
2	bay leaves, crushed	2
½ tsp	thyme	2 mL
2	garlic cloves, peeled, crushed and chopped	2
	salt and pepper	
	lemon juice	
	Barbecue Sauce for Brochettes (see page 95)	

1 Place sausages, bell pepper, cheese and tomatoes in bowl. Add oil, seasonings, garlic and lemon juice. Mix well, cover and marinate 1 hour in refrigerator. Reserve marinade.

2 Thread ingredients alternately on short wooden skewers. Season generously and grill on barbecue about 6 minutes, turning frequently. Baste with leftover marinade during cooking.

3 Serve with barbecue sauce.

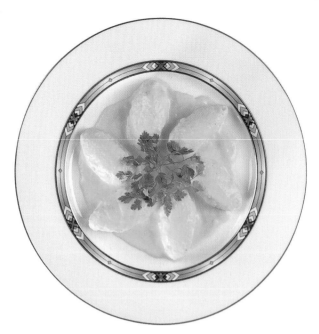

Chicken Quenelles
(4 to 8 servings)

2	whole boneless chicken breasts, skinned	2
2	egg whites	2
2 tbsp	chopped fresh basil	30 mL
2½ cups	heavy cream	625 mL
4 cups	light chicken stock	1 L
3	yellow bell peppers, halved and seeded	3
	salt and freshly ground pepper	
	cayenne pepper to taste	

1 Dice chicken meat and place in food processor. Add egg whites and blend until mixture can be forced through coarse sieve.

2 When mixture has been passed through sieve into bowl, cover with plastic wrap and refrigerate 2 hours.

3 Place chicken mixture in food processor and begin mixing at low speed. Add basil, salt, pepper and cayenne pepper to taste.

4 Gradually add 1½ cups (375 mL) cream while mixing at low speed. The mixture must become homogeneous. Add more cream if necessary. Shape mixture into small quenelles (dumplings).

5 Bring chicken stock to simmer in saucepan. Add quenelles and cook in hot liquid. When quenelles rise to surface, remove and drain on paper towels.

6 Blanch bell peppers 5 minutes in salted, boiling water. Remove, peel and purée in food processor.

7 Place pepper purée in sauté pan and season well. Cook 3 minutes at medium heat. Reduce heat to low, pour in remaining cream and cook 4 minutes.

8 Add quenelles and simmer 2 minutes. Serve.

Dice chicken meat and place in food processor. Add egg whites and blend.

Pass mixture through coarse sieve into bowl.

Place cooked chicken mixture in food processor and begin mixing at low speed. Add basil, salt, pepper and cayenne pepper to taste.

Gradually add 1½ cups (375 mL) cream while mixing at low speed.

Bring chicken stock to simmer in saucepan. Add quenelles and cook in hot liquid.

Stuffed Fresh Clams
(6 to 8 servings)

24 – 32	fresh clams, scrubbed	24 – 32
3	anchovy fillets, drained and puréed	3
5	blanched garlic cloves, puréed	5
½ lb	softened butter	225 g
1	dry shallot, peeled and chopped	1
2 tbsp	chopped fresh parsley	30 mL
½ cup	breadcrumbs	125 mL
	lemon juice	
	salt and freshly ground pepper	

Preheat oven to 400°F (200°C).

1 Place clams in large saucepan and pour in 1½ cups (375 mL) water. Add lemon juice, cover and bring to boiling point. Cook 3 minutes or until shells open. Remove clams from pan, discarding any unopened shells.

2 Detach clams from shells, without removing, and set aside.

3 Mix remaining ingredients, except breadcrumbs, in small bowl. Cover clams with butter mixture, then sprinkle with breadcrumbs.

4 Cook 6 minutes in oven and serve. Garnish with additional anchovy fillets, if desired.

Ratatouille on Toast
(4 to 6 servings)

3 tbsp	olive oil	45 mL
1	large onion, peeled and thinly sliced	1
1	large eggplant	1
1	green bell pepper, thinly sliced	1
1	yellow bell pepper, thinly sliced	1
1	zucchini, sliced	1
3	garlic cloves, peeled, crushed and chopped	3
3 tbsp	chopped fresh parsley	45 mL
1 tbsp	chopped fresh basil	15 mL
2	tomatoes, peeled, seeded and chopped	2
1½ cups	grated Gruyère cheese	375 mL
	salt and pepper	
	slices of toasted French bread	

Preheat oven to 375°F (190°C).

1 Heat oil in large sauté pan over medium heat. Add onion, season and cook 16 minutes over low heat, stirring occasionally.

2 Meanwhile, cut eggplant in half lengthwise. Score flesh and place, skin-side-up, on cookie sheet. Bake 30 minutes. Scoop out flesh and set aside.

3 Add bell peppers, zucchini, garlic, and herbs to cooking onion. Season well and mix. Continue cooking 18 minutes over low heat.

4 Mix in eggplant and tomatoes; season well. Cook 15 minutes.

5 Spread ratatouille on toast and sprinkle with cheese. Broil 8 minutes in oven until golden brown and serve.

Browned Mussels in the Shell
(4 to 6 servings)

4½ lb	mussels, bearded and scrubbed	2 kg
½ cup	dry white wine	125 mL
4 tbsp	olive oil	60 mL
2 cups	homemade white breadcrumbs	500 mL
4	garlic cloves, peeled, crushed and chopped	4
2 tbsp	chopped fresh parsley	30 mL
1 tbsp	chopped fresh tarragon	15 mL
	juice of ½ lemon	
	salt and freshly ground pepper	

Preheat oven to 425°F (220°C).

1 Place mussels in large pot. Add wine, lemon juice and pepper. Cover and bring to boil. Cook mussels over low heat until shells open, about 5 minutes. Stir once during cooking.

2 Remove mussels from pot, discarding any unopened shells. Arrange mussels on the half shell in ovenproof platter. Pass cooking liquid through sieve lined with cheesecloth. Set aside.

3 Heat oil in frying pan over medium heat. Add breadcrumbs, garlic and herbs; season well. Cook 2 minutes over medium heat, stirring to prevent burning.

4 Sprinkle breadcrumb mixture over mussels and drizzle with cooking liquid. Cook 8 minutes in oven and serve.

Oysters with Fresh Spinach
(4 to 6 servings)

12 to 18	fresh oysters, scrubbed and opened	12 to 18
¼ cup	butter	50 mL
½ cup	chopped dry shallots	125 mL
¼ cup	chopped fresh parsley	50 mL
¼ cup	chopped fresh chives	50 mL
1 cup	chopped fresh spinach	250 mL
¼ cup	white breadcrumbs	50 mL
	salt and pepper	

Preheat oven to 400°F (200°C).

1 Arrange oysters on the half shell on oyster plates. Be careful to keep juice in shell.

2 Heat butter in frying pan over medium heat. Add shallots, fresh herbs and spinach. Season well and cook 5 minutes over low heat.

3 Mix in breadcrumbs and remove pan from heat. Spread mixture over oysters and bake 8 minutes. Serve.

* If desired, the topping ingredients can be doubled for more servings.

Cheese-Stuffed Hard-Boiled Eggs
(4 to 6 servings)

6	hard-boiled eggs	6
1 tbsp	Dijon mustard	15 mL
2 tbsp	soft cream cheese	30 mL
¼ cup	mayonnaise	50 mL
	salt and pepper	
	Worcestershire sauce to taste	
	lemon juice	
	lettuce leaves	
	chopped fresh parsley	

1 Peel eggs and slice in half. Remove yolks carefully and place in wire sieve. Force through into bowl. Reserve white shells.

2 Add mustard, cheese and mayonnaise to egg yolks. Mix very well and season with salt and pepper. Add Worcestershire sauce and lemon juice. Mix again.

3 Line serving platter with lettuce leaves. Using pastry bag fitted with star tip, stuff egg white shells with yolk mixture. Arrange on serving platter and sprinkle with chopped parsley.

Sweet and Sour Chicken Drumsticks
(4 to 6 servings)

2 lb	lean chicken drumsticks	900 g
1 tbsp	olive oil	15 mL
½ cup	honey	125 mL
3 tbsp	soy sauce	45 mL
2 tbsp	white vinegar	30 mL
2 tbsp	teriyaki sauce	30 mL
3	garlic cloves, peeled and sliced	3
1 tbsp	chopped fresh ginger	15 mL
	salt and freshly ground pepper	
	cayenne pepper to taste	

Preheat oven to 325°F (160°C).

1 Place drumsticks in saucepan and cover with water. Cook 18 minutes over medium heat. Drain well and remove skin.

2 Heat oil in large ovenproof sauté pan over medium heat. Mix remaining ingredients together in small bowl. Add drumsticks to hot oil and pour in sauce. Season generously.

3 Bake 40 minutes in oven or adjust time according to size. Do not cover. Stir during cooking.

Eggplant-Stuffed Mushrooms au Gratin
(4 to 6 servings)

1	large eggplant	1
3 tbsp	butter	45 mL
2	garlic cloves, peeled, crushed and chopped	2
1 tbsp	chopped fresh basil	15 mL
¼ tsp	thyme	1 mL
1 tbsp	curry powder	15 mL
3 tbsp	flour	45 mL
1½ cups	milk, heated	375 mL
¼ tsp	nutmeg	1 mL
2 tbsp	olive oil	30 mL
24	large fresh mushroom caps, cleaned	24
1½ cups	grated Swiss cheese	375 mL
	salt and pepper	

Preheat oven to 375°F (190°C).

1 Cut eggplant in half lengthwise. Score flesh and place, skin-side-up, on cookie sheet. Bake 45 minutes. Scoop out flesh and set aside.

2 Increase oven setting to 400°F (200°C).

3 Heat butter in saucepan over medium heat. Add eggplant, garlic, basil, thyme and curry powder; mix well. Season with salt and pepper; cook 3 minutes.

4 Sprinkle in flour and mix well. Cook 1 minute. Incorporate milk and nutmeg; season well. Cook 6 minutes over low heat. Set aside.

5 Heat oil in frying pan over medium heat. Add mushroom caps and sauté 4 minutes. Transfer mushroom caps to baking dish and stuff with eggplant mixture.

6 Top with cheese and bake 8 minutes. Serve.

Cut eggplant in half lengthwise. Score flesh and place, skin-side-up, on cookie sheet.

Heat butter in saucepan over medium heat. Add eggplant, garlic, basil, thyme and curry powder; mix well. Season with salt and pepper; cook 3 minutes.

Sprinkle in flour and mix well. Cook 1 minute. Incorporate milk and nutmeg; season well. Cook 6 minutes over low heat.

Heat oil in frying pan over medium heat. Add mushroom caps and sauté 4 minutes.

Stuff mushroom caps with eggplant mixture.

Crabmeat Gourmet
(4 to 6 servings)

2 tbsp	olive oil	30 mL
2	dry shallots, peeled and chopped	2
1	garlic clove, peeled, crushed and chopped	1
1 tbsp	chopped fresh basil	15 mL
2	tomatoes, peeled, seeded and chopped	2
3 tbsp	tarragon wine vinegar	45 mL
2 tbsp	capers	30 mL
1 tbsp	chopped anchovies	15 mL
½ cup	mayonnaise	125 mL
¾ lb	fresh crabmeat, cooked	350 g
	salt and freshly ground pepper	
	lemon juice	

1 Heat oil in frying pan over medium heat. Add shallots, garlic and basil; cook 3 minutes. Add tomatoes and vinegar; season well. Cook 12 minutes over medium heat.

2 Remove pan from heat and let mixture cool. Purée in food processor and transfer to bowl.

3 Add capers, anchovies and mayonnaise; mix well. Season and add lemon juice to taste.

4 Mix in crabmeat and spread on toasted bread and crackers.

Chicken Cheese Spread
(10 to 12 servings)

1	whole boneless chicken breast	1
½	celery rib, sliced	½
1	small onion, peeled and sliced	1
2 tbsp	curry powder	30 mL
2 tbsp	chopped pimiento pepper	30 mL
½ cup	chopped almonds	125 mL
2	dry shallots, peeled and chopped	2
1	garlic clove, peeled, crushed and chopped	1
6 oz	cream cheese	175 g
1 tbsp	sour cream	15 mL
	salt and pepper	

1 Skin chicken breast and split in half. Place in sauté pan with celery, onion and half of curry powder. Pour in enough cold water to cover and season well. Bring to boil. Reduce heat to low and cook 12 minutes or adjust time according to size.

2 Remove chicken from liquid and let cool.

3 Dice chicken meat finely and place in food processor. Add remaining ingredients and blend until well combined. If mixture is not soft enough, add more sour cream. Serve as a spread for canapés.

Broiled Mushrooms on Baguette
(6 to 10 servings)

1 lb	fresh mushrooms, cleaned and finely chopped	450 g
3 tbsp	olive oil	45 mL
3	dry shallots, peeled and finely chopped	3
2	garlic cloves, peeled, crushed and finely chopped	2
½ cup	heavy cream	125 mL
1 cup	grated Gruyère cheese	250 mL
	salt and freshly ground pepper	
	slices of toasted French baguette	
	cayenne pepper to taste	
	pinch of paprika	

1 Place chopped mushrooms in clean towel and squeeze out juice. Heat oil in sauté pan over medium heat. Add mushrooms, shallots, and garlic; cook until moisture evaporates.

2 Pour in cream, mix and cook 4 minutes. Season well and spread mixture on toast. Top with cheese and broil in oven 2 minutes.

3 Sprinkle with cayenne pepper and paprika. Serve.

Canapés Florentine
(6 to 10 servings)

3 tbsp	butter	45 mL
2	dry shallots, peeled and chopped	2
1	garlic clove, peeled, crushed and chopped	1
2	bunches fresh spinach, well cleaned, cooked and finely chopped	2
1	recipe Extra Thick White Sauce, heated (see page 94)	1
4	slices crisp cooked bacon	4
1 cup	grated Gruyère cheese	250 mL
	slices of toasted French bread	
	salt and freshly ground pepper	
	cayenne pepper to taste	

1 Remove crusts from bread and square off ends. Cut into triangles and set aside.

2 Heat butter in sauté pan over medium heat. Add shallots, garlic and spinach; season well. Cook 3 minutes over high heat.

3 Stir in white sauce and season with cayenne pepper. Spread mixture on bread triangles. Top each with bacon and cheese.

4 Broil 4 minutes in preheated oven. Serve hot.

Zesty Meatballs
(6 to 8 servings)

1 lb	lean ground beef	450 g
½ cup	minced cooked onion	125 mL
4	blanched garlic cloves, puréed	4
¼ cup	grated Parmesan cheese	50 mL
1	egg, beaten	1
1 tbsp	olive oil	15 mL
	pinch crushed chilies	
	salt and freshly ground pepper	
	few drops of Tabasco sauce	
	oil for frying	

1 Place all ingredients in food processor. Blend together until well combined.

2 Grease hands with oil and shape meat into small meatballs.

3 Fry meatballs in hot oil over medium heat in several batches. Drain on paper towels. Serve with spicy dipping sauces.

Cheese Fritters
(4 to 6 servings)

1 cup	water	250 mL
6 tbsp	butter	90 mL
1 cup	all-purpose flour	250 mL
4	large eggs	4
½ lb	grated Parmesan cheese	225 g
	pinch of salt	
	freshly ground pepper	
	cayenne pepper to taste	
	oil for deep-frying	

1 Place water, butter and salt in saucepan. Bring to boil. As soon as butter is melted, add flour. Stir quickly with wooden spoon, mixing until batter no longer sticks to sides of pan.

2 Remove pan from heat and transfer mixture to food processor. Add one egg at a time, blending well between additions.

3 Add cheese and season with salt, pepper and cayenne pepper. Blend briefly, just to incorporate.

4 Drop small spoonfuls of batter into hot oil. Deep-fry until golden brown. Drain on paper towels before serving.

Stuffed Eggs with Anchovies
(4 to 6 servings)

8	hard-boiled eggs	8
6	anchovy fillets, drained and puréed	6
4 tbsp	mayonnaise	60 mL
I tbsp	Dijon mustard	15 mL
	salt and freshly ground pepper	
	lemon juice to taste	
	few drops of Worcestershire sauce	
	cayenne pepper to taste	
	lettuce leaves	

1 Peel eggs and slice in half. Remove yolks carefully and place in wire sieve. Force through into bowl.

2 Add puréed anchovies, mayonnaise and mustard to egg yolks. Mix well and season generously. Add lemon juice, Worcestershire sauce and cayenne pepper. Mix again.

3 Line serving platter with lettuce leaves. Using pastry bag fitted with star tip, stuff yolk mixture into egg white shells. Arrange on serving platter.

4 Sprinkle with cayenne pepper and serve. Garnish with chopped anchovies, if desired.

Seafood and Tomato Tartlets
(4 to 6 servings)

1 tbsp	olive oil	15 mL
½ lb	fresh shrimp, peeled and deveined	225 g
1	garlic clove, peeled, crushed and chopped	1
2	dry shallots, peeled and chopped	2
2	tomatoes, peeled, seeded and chopped	2
1 tbsp	chopped fresh basil	15 mL
6	tartlets, precooked	6
1 cup	grated mozzarella cheese	250 mL
	salt and freshly ground pepper	

Preheat oven to 400°F (200°C).

1 Heat oil in frying pan over medium heat. Add shrimp and season well; cook 2 minutes on each side. Remove shrimp from pan and set aside.

2 Add garlic, shallots, tomatoes and basil to hot pan. Season well and cook 4 minutes over high heat.

3 Coarsely chop shrimp and arrange in tartlets. Top with tomato mixture and cover with cheese. Season well with pepper.

4 Brown 8 minutes in oven. Serve hot. Garnish with whole shrimp, if desired.

Marinated Beef Strips on French Baguette
(6 to 8 servings)

5 tbsp	olive oil	75 mL
2	strip loin steaks, ¾ in (2 cm) thick	2
2	dry shallots, peeled and chopped	2
2	garlic cloves, peeled and thinly sliced	2
1 tbsp	chopped fresh basil	15 mL
1 tbsp	chopped fresh parsley	15 mL
½	jalapeño pepper, seeded and chopped	½
2 tbsp	red wine vinegar	30 mL
	salt and freshly ground pepper	
	Dijon mustard	
	slices of toasted French baguette	

1 Heat 1 tbsp (15 mL) oil in frying pan over medium heat. When very hot, add steaks and cook 3 minutes on one side. Turn meat over, season well and continue cooking 3 minutes.

2 Remove steaks from pan and set aside on cutting board. Mix remaining ingredients, except mustard and bread, together in small bowl.

3 Slice steaks thinly and arrange on serving platter. Pour sauce over meat and marinate 1 hour in refrigerator.

4 To serve, spread mustard on slices of toasted baguette. Top with several slices of marinated beef and season well with pepper.

Tangy Roquefort Spread
(4 to 6 servings)

1	red bell pepper	1
2	garlic cloves	2
⅓ lb	Roquefort cheese	150 g
⅓ lb	soft cream cheese	150 g
	few drops of Tabasco sauce	
	freshly ground pepper	

1 Cut bell pepper in half and re-move seeds. Oil skin and place cut-side-down on cookie sheet; broil 6 minutes in oven. Remove from oven and let cool. Peel off skin, slice pepper and mash.

2 Place garlic cloves in salted, boiling water. Blanch 4 minutes. Peel and purée.

3 Place all ingredients in food processor. Blend to obtain smooth consistency.

4 Spread on toast, crackers or serve with crudités.

Zucchini Boats Stuffed with Fresh Salmon
(4 servings)

4	small zucchini	4
6 oz	fresh salmon, cooked and flaked	175 g
1	shallot, peeled and chopped	1
1 tbsp	chopped fresh basil	15 mL
1 tbsp	chopped fresh dill	15 mL
3 tbsp	mayonnaise	45 mL
	salt and pepper	
	lemon juice	
	chopped fresh parsley	
	lemon wedges	

1 Cut zucchini in half lengthwise. Hollow out leaving sturdy shell. Place in salted, boiling water and blanch 5 minutes. Remove and cool under cold, running water. Drain well and set aside on paper towels.

2 Place remaining ingredients, except parsley and lemon wedges, in bowl. Mix together gently and correct seasoning. Fill zucchini boats with mixture.

3 Sprinkle with chopped parsley and serve with lemon wedges.

Baked Endives with Ham and Cheese
(4 servings)

2 tbsp	butter	30 mL
4	large Belgian endives, cored	4
¼ cup	dry white wine	50 mL
½ cup	water	125 mL
4	large slices cooked ham	4
4	large slices Gruyère or Swiss cheese	4
	juice of ½ lemon	
	salt and freshly ground pepper	
	paprika to taste	
	chopped fresh parsley	

Preheat oven to 400°F (200°C).

1 Heat butter in sauté pan over medium heat. Add endives and cook 3 minutes.

2 Pour in wine, water and lemon juice. Season with salt and pepper. Cover and cook 15 minutes over medium heat or adjust time according to size. Endives must be fully cooked.

3 Remove endives, reserving liquid, and pat dry with paper towels. Wrap each endive in slice of ham, then in slice of cheese. Secure with toothpicks if necessary.

4 Pour small amount of cooking liquid in bottom of small baking dish. Arrange endives in dish, sprinkle with paprika and place in oven. Bake 10 minutes or until cheese is golden brown.

5 Sprinkle with chopped fresh parsley and serve.

Chicken Liver Pâté
(6 to 8 servings)

¼ lb	butter	125 g
2	dry shallots, peeled and chopped	2
1	small onion, peeled and chopped	1
¾ lb	chicken livers, cleaned and halved	350 g
1 tbsp	chopped fresh tarragon	15 mL
¼ tsp	thyme	1 mL
3 tbsp	brandy	45 mL
½ cup	heavy cream, whipped	125 mL
	salt and freshly ground pepper	
	cayenne pepper to taste	

1 Heat butter in frying pan over medium heat. Add shallots and onion; cook 4 minutes.

2 Add chicken livers and season well. Sprinkle in herbs and cook 4 to 5 minutes or until liver turns grey. Pour in brandy and cook 1 minute over high heat.

3 Remove pan from heat and force mixture through sieve into bowl. Season purée well and incorporate whipped cream.

4 Transfer mixture to clean bowl and cover with plastic wrap. Refrigerate 2 hours.

5 Serve pâté in small bowl and accompany with toasted bread and pickles.

Heat butter in frying pan over medium heat. Add shallots and onion; cook 4 minutes.

Add chicken livers and season well. Sprinkle in herbs and cook 4 to 5 minutes or until liver turns grey.

Pour in brandy and cook 1 minute over high heat.

Remove pan from heat and force mixture through sieve into bowl.

Season purée well and incorporate whipped cream.

Easy Seafood Appetizer
(6 to 8 servings)

3 tbsp	butter	45 mL
3	green onions, chopped	3
2	garlic cloves, peeled, crushed and chopped	2
1 tbsp	chopped fresh basil	15 mL
12	shrimp, peeled and deveined	12
12	slices toasted French baguette	12
	salt and freshly ground pepper	

1 Heat butter in frying pan over medium heat. Add green onions, garlic and basil. Cook 1 minute.

2 Add shrimp and season well. Sauté 3 minutes.

3 Place one shrimp on each slice of bread. Serve.

Tender Deep-Fried Sole
(6 to 8 servings)

3	large sole fillets	3
⅓ cup	grated Parmesan cheese	75 mL
½ cup	seasoned flour	125 mL
2	eggs, beaten	2
1 cup	breadcrumbs	250 mL
	cayenne pepper	
	juice of 1 lemon	
	tartar sauce	

1 Cut fillets into sticks. Place cheese in large plate. Season with cayenne pepper and coat fish in mixture. Dredge fish in flour.

2 Dip fish in beaten eggs and coat in breadcrumbs. Deep-fry in hot oil 1 minute. Drain on paper towels and serve with lemon juice. Accompany with tartar sauce.

Vegetable-Stuffed Artichoke Bottoms
(4 servings)

8	cooked artichoke bottoms	8
l cup	diced cooked potatoes	250 mL
l cup	diced cooked carrots	250 mL
½ cup	cooked peas	125 mL
½ cup	diced cooked green beans	125 mL
l cup	canned crabmeat	250 mL
l tbsp	chopped fresh basil	15 mL
l	dry shallot, peeled and chopped	l
⅓ cup	mayonnaise	75 mL
l tsp	Dijon mustard	5 mL
	lemon juice	
	salt and freshly ground pepper	
	pinch of paprika	
	few drops of Tabasco sauce	

1 Arrange artichoke bottoms on serving platter. Sprinkle with lemon juice and season well.

2 Mix vegetables, crabmeat, basil and shallot together in bowl. Add mayonnaise and mustard; mix well. Add all seasonings and mix again.

3 Stuff artichoke bottoms, sprinkle with paprika and serve.

Celery Sticks Stuffed with Saint-André Cheese
(6 to 10 servings)

⅓ lb	blue cheese	150 g
⅓ lb	soft cream cheese	150 g
⅓ lb	Saint-André cheese	150 g
2 tbsp	sour cream	30 mL
	salt and freshly ground pepper	
	cayenne pepper to taste	
	celery ribs	
	shredded lettuce	

1 Place all cheeses and sour cream in food processor. Blend until well incorporated. Season with salt, pepper and cayenne pepper. Add more sour cream if mixture is too thick. Blend briefly.

2 Spoon mixture into pastry bag fitted with star tip. Stuff celery ribs and arrange on platter. Cover with plastic wrap and refrigerate 1 hour.

3 To serve, cut stuffed celery ribs into 1-in (2.5-cm) pieces. Arrange on serving platter lined with shredded lettuce.

Spicy Pork Spareribs
(6 to 8 servings)

SPARERIBS:

5 lb	lean pork spareribs	2.3 kg
1	onion, peeled and quartered	1
1	carrot, pared and sliced	1
1	celery rib, sliced	1
2	bay leaves	2
	fresh thyme	
	salt and freshly ground pepper	
	cayenne pepper and paprika to taste	

1 Place all ingredients in roasting pan and pour in enough cold water to barely cover. Cook 30 minutes over medium heat.

2 Remove spareribs from pan and cut in half. Set ribs aside in deep platter.

SAUCE:

¼ cup	soy sauce	50 mL
2 tbsp	teriyaki sauce	30 mL
¼ cup	brown sugar	50 mL
2	garlic cloves, peeled and sliced	2
¼ cup	dry white wine	50 mL
1 tbsp	chopped fresh ginger	15 mL
1	jalapeño pepper, seeded and chopped	1
¼ tsp	allspice	1 mL
¼ tsp	nutmeg	1 mL

1 Place all ingredients in saucepan and cook 3 minutes or until sugar dissolves. Pour over ribs and marinate 15 minutes.

2 Remove spareribs from marinade and grill on barbecue 20 to 25 minutes or adjust time according to size. Turn ribs over frequently during cooking and baste with marinade.

Shrimp Croquettes
(4 to 6 servings)

1 tbsp	butter	15 mL
1	shallot, peeled and chopped	1
¾ lb	fresh shrimp, peeled, deveined and chopped	350 g
¾ cup	Extra Thick White Sauce, heated (see page 94)	175 mL
¾ cup	flour	175 mL
2	eggs, beaten	2
¾ cup	breadcrumbs	175 mL
	salt and freshly ground pepper	
	cayenne pepper to taste	
	oil for deep-frying	

1 Heat butter in saucepan over medium heat. Add shallot and shrimp; season with salt, pepper and cayenne pepper. Cook 2 minutes.

2 Stir in white sauce. Increase heat to high and cook 2 minutes, stirring constantly. Pour mixture onto serving platter and cool in refrigerator.

3 Shape mixture into bite size croquettes. Dredge in flour, dip in beaten eggs and roll in breadcrumbs.

4 Deep-fry in hot oil until golden brown. Drain on paper towels and serve.

Artichoke Soufflé
(6 servings)

12	cooked artichoke bottoms	12
2 tbsp	butter	30 mL
2 tbsp	flour	30 mL
1 cup	milk, heated	250 mL
3	egg yolks	3
½ cup	grated Gruyère cheese	125 mL
4	egg whites, beaten stiff	4
	salt and pepper	

Preheat oven to 375°F (190°C).

1 Arrange artichoke bottoms in single layer in buttered baking dish. Season well and set aside.

2 Heat butter in saucepan over medium heat. Sprinkle in flour and mix well. Pour in milk, season and whisk to incorporate. Cook sauce 6 minutes.

3 Remove saucepan from heat and whisk in egg yolks. Add cheese, season and mix well. Fold in beaten egg whites.

4 Pour batter into artichoke bottoms in baking dish. Cook 12 minutes in oven. Serve at once.

Broiled Littleneck Clams with Herb Butter
(4 servings)

¼ lb	softened unsalted butter	125 g
2 tbsp	chopped fresh parsley	30 mL
½ tsp	oregano	2 mL
1 tsp	chopped fresh chives	5 mL
2	garlic cloves, peeled, crushed and chopped	2
2 tbsp	brandy	30 mL
1 tsp	Worcestershire sauce	5 mL
24	littleneck clams, scrubbed and opened	24
½ cup	white breadcrumbs	125 mL
	salt and freshly ground pepper	

1 Place butter, fresh herbs and seasonings in bowl. Add garlic, brandy and Worcestershire sauce. Mix together until well combined.

2 Mound butter on large sheet of doubled foil. Form butter into cylindrical shape and roll up in foil. Twist ends shut.

3 Chill 1 hour in refrigerator.

4 Arrange clams on the half shell in baking dish. Top each with slice of herbed butter and sprinkle with breadcrumbs.

5 Broil 3 minutes in oven and serve.

Oysters on the Half Shell
(4 servings)

24	fresh oysters, scrubbed and opened	24
3	dry shallots, peeled and chopped	3
¼ cup	wine vinegar	50 mL
½ cup	catsup	125 mL
3 tbsp	chili sauce	45 mL
1 tbsp	horseradish	15 mL
	lemon juice	
	few drops of Worcestershire sauce	
	freshly ground pepper	
	thin slices of pumpernickel bread, buttered	

1 Arrange oysters on the half shell on oyster plates. Be careful to keep juice in shell.

2 Mix shallots, wine vinegar and lemon juice together. Set sauce aside.

3 Mix catsup, chili sauce, horse-radish, lemon juice and Worcestershire sauce together. Season well with pepper. Set aside.

4 Serve oysters with sauces and accompany with bread.

Cheese Balls Spiked with Wine
(6 to 8 servings)

½ cup	dry white wine	125 mL
½ lb	grated Gruyère cheese	225 g
½ cup	all-purpose flour	125 mL
2	eggs, beaten	2
½ cup	breadcrumbs	125 mL
	freshly ground pepper	
	dash of paprika	
	cayenne pepper to taste	
	oil for deep-frying	

1 Pour wine into saucepan and cook over medium heat. When liquid is hot, add grated cheese and all seasonings. Continue cooking 3 to 4 minutes until mixture becomes creamy.

2 Remove saucepan from heat and pour mixture into deep serving platter. Let cool, then shape into small balls.

3 Dredge cheese balls in flour, dip in beaten eggs and coat thoroughly in breadcrumbs.

4 Deep-fry in hot oil until golden; about 1 minute. Drain on paper towels and serve.

Croque-Monsieur
(4 to 6 servings)

4	large slices cooked ham	4
8	large slices Gruyère cheese	8
8	slices French bread	8
3	eggs, beaten	3
2 tbsp	butter	30 mL
	freshly ground pepper	

1 Make sandwiches with one slice of ham between two slices of cheese. Season generously with pepper. Dip sandwiches in beaten eggs.

2 Heat butter in large frying pan over medium heat. Fry sandwiches about 3 to 4 minutes on each side until golden brown. Slice and serve.

Shrimp with Brandy
(4 servings)

12	large fresh shrimp	12
½ cup	flour	125 mL
2	eggs, beaten	2
2 tbsp	brandy	30 mL
	lemon juice	
	salt and pepper	
	oil for deep-frying	

1 Peel shrimp leaving tails intact. Using tip of paring knife, remove dark dorsal vein. Place in bowl and season well. Add lemon juice, toss and set aside.

2 Place flour, pinch of salt and eggs in bowl. Mix together and add brandy. If batter is too thick, add some cold water.

3 Dip shrimp in batter and deep-fry in hot oil until golden brown. Serve with a spicy dipping sauce.

Lobster Canapés Supreme
(4 to 6 servings)

3 tbsp	butter	45 mL
2	dry shallots, peeled and chopped	2
4	watercress sprigs, chopped	4
1 tbsp	chopped fresh parsley	15 mL
2 tbsp	flour	30 mL
1½ cups	light cream	375 mL
¾ lb	chopped cooked lobster meat	350 g
½ cup	white breadcrumbs	125 mL
	salt and pepper	
	pinch of paprika	
	slices of toasted French baguette	

1 Heat butter in saucepan over medium heat. Add shallots, watercress and parsley; cook 2 minutes. Mix in flour and cook 30 seconds.

2 Incorporate cream, season well and cook sauce 6 minutes over low heat. Stir in lobster meat and continue cooking 1 minute.

3 Season with paprika and spread mixture over toasted bread. Place slices on cookie sheet and top with breadcrumbs. Broil 2 minutes in oven and serve.

Cauliflower with Garlic Mayonnaise
(6 to 8 servings)

1	medium cauliflower, cooked al dente	1
2	egg yolks	2
5	blanched garlic cloves, puréed	5
1 tbsp	lemon juice	15 mL
1 cup	olive oil	250 mL
1 tbsp	white wine vinegar	15 mL
½ cup	black pitted olives, chopped	125 mL
	salt and pepper	
	chopped fresh basil, parsley and chives	

1 Separate cauliflower into florets and arrange on serving platter. Set aside.

2 Place egg yolks, garlic and lemon juice in bowl. Mix well. Incorporate olive oil gradually, beginning with thin stream. Whisk constantly. As soon as mayonnaise thickens, increase flow of oil. When all of oil is incorporated, season generously.

3 Whisk in vinegar and correct seasoning. Pour mayonnaise over cauliflower. Sprinkle with olives and chopped fresh herbs.

4 Serve at room temperature.

Asparagus en Croûte
(4 servings)

16	asparagus stalks, cooked	16
4	slices French bread	4
4	slices prosciutto ham	4
½ cup	white sauce, heated (see page 94)	125 mL
1 cup	grated Gruyère cheese	250 mL
	salt and freshly ground pepper	
	pinch of paprika	

1 Toast bread on one side only. Square off sides and ends. Cover toasted side with slice of ham.

2 Cut asparagus stalks to fit bread and position neatly. Measure from tips of stalk, trimming off excess from base end.

3 Arrange in large baking dish and top with white sauce. Season well with salt, pepper and paprika. Cover with cheese.

4 Broil 6 minutes in oven until golden brown. Serve.

Baked Tomatoes Stuffed with Mushrooms
(4 servings)

4	large tomatoes	4
2 tbsp	olive oil	30 mL
½ lb	fresh mushrooms, cleaned and finely chopped	225 g
2	dry shallots, peeled and chopped	2
2	garlic cloves, peeled, crushed and chopped	2
1 tbsp	chopped fresh basil	15 mL
4	anchovy fillets, drained and finely chopped	4
½ cup	white breadcrumbs	125 mL
	salt and pepper	

Preheat oven to 350°F (180°C).

1 Slice top off tomatoes and re-move most of pulp with spoon. Season cavities well and add few drops of oil. Set tomatoes aside, reserving pulp.

2 Heat remaining oil in frying pan over medium heat. Add mush-rooms, shallots, garlic and basil; season well. Cook 3 minutes over high heat. Stir in anchovies and continue cooking 2 minutes.

3 Add tomato pulp to mushroom mixture. Correct seasoning and cook 2 minutes over high heat.

4 Fill tomatoes with mixture. Sprin-kle with breadcrumbs and place in baking dish. Bake 18 minutes or adjust time according to size of tomatoes.

Slice top off tomatoes and remove most of pulp with spoon.

Season cavities well and add few drops of oil.

Heat remaining oil in frying pan over medium heat. Add mushrooms, shallots, garlic and basil; season well. Cook 3 minutes.

Add tomato pulp to mushroom mixture. Correct seasoning and cook 2 minutes over high heat.

Fill tomatoes with mixture.

Asparagus Tartlets au Gratin
(4 to 6 servings)

1	bunch fresh asparagus	1
6	tartlets, precooked	6
1½ cups	Basic White Sauce, heated (see page 94)	375 mL
1 cup	grated Gruyère cheese	250 mL
	salt and freshly ground pepper	
	paprika to taste	

Preheat oven to 400°F (200°C).

1 Pare asparagus if necessary and trim base ends. Cook stalks in salted, boiling water until tender. Drain well and pat dry with paper towels.

2 Cut asparagus stalks into small pieces and arrange in tartlets. Place molds on cookie sheet.

3 Add white sauce and top with cheese. Season with salt, pepper and paprika. Brown 8 minutes in oven. Serve hot.

Anchovy and Mushroom Tartlets
(4 to 6 servings)

2 tbsp	butter	30 mL
6	anchovy fillets, drained and finely chopped	6
2	dry shallots, peeled and finely chopped	2
1	small onion, peeled and chopped	1
½ lb	fresh mushrooms, cleaned and diced	225 g
1 tbsp	chopped fresh chives	15 mL
1 cup	Basic White Sauce, heated (see page 94)	250 mL
6	tartlets, precooked	6
½ cup	grated Gruyère cheese	125 mL
	pinch of curry powder	
	salt and freshly ground pepper	

Preheat oven to 400°F (200°C).

1 Heat butter in frying pan over medium heat. Add chopped anchovies, shallots and onion; cook 2 minutes.

2 Add mushrooms, chives and curry powder. Season well and mix. Cook 4 minutes over medium heat.

3 Stir in white sauce and cook 1 minute. Fill tartlets with mixture and top with cheese. Brown 6 minutes in oven and serve hot. Garnish with anchovy fillets, if desired.

Muscovite Tomatoes
(4 to 6 servings)

8	Italian tomatoes	8
4	hard-boiled eggs	4
5	anchovy fillets, drained and finely chopped	5
1 tbsp	Dijon mustard	15 mL
1 tsp	Worcestershire sauce	5 mL
1 tbsp	wine vinegar	15 mL
4 tbsp	olive oil	60 mL
	salt and pepper	
	lemon juice to taste	

1 Cut tomatoes in half lengthwise and remove most of pulp with spoon. Season cavities well and add few drops of oil. Set aside.

2 Peel eggs and slice in half. Remove yolks carefully and place in wire sieve. Force through into bowl. Set whites aside for other uses.

3 Add anchovies, mustard, Worcestershire sauce and vinegar to egg yolks. Mix very well. Incorporate oil in thin stream while blending together.

4 Season well and add lemon juice. Fill tomatoes with mixture and serve.

Melon with Roquefort Cheese in Port
(4 to 6 servings)

1	small honeydew melon	1
4 tbsp	port wine	60 mL
⅓ lb	Roquefort cheese	150 g
	freshly ground pepper	
	fresh mint leaves	

1 Cut melon in half and remove seeds. Using melon baller, cut flesh and place in bowl. Add wine and marinate 15 minutes.

2 Chop cheese into small pieces and add to bowl. Mix well, season with pepper and serve in small bowls. Garnish with fresh mint.

Fresh Oysters au Gratin
(6 to 8 servings)

24	fresh oysters, scrubbed and opened	24
1½ cups	white coarse breadcrumbs	375 mL
1 cup	grated Parmesan cheese	250 mL
⅓ cup	melted butter	75 mL
	rock salt	
	freshly ground pepper	
	cayenne pepper to taste	

1 Arrange oysters on the shell on tray lined with rock salt.

2 Mix breadcrumbs with cheese and seasonings. Sprinkle over oysters. Drizzle melted butter over topping.

3 Broil oysters until nicely browned and serve.

Chopped Egg Canapés
(8 to 10 servings)

6	large hard-boiled eggs	6
1 tbsp	Dijon mustard	15 mL
3 tbsp	mayonnaise	45 mL
¼ cup	chopped pimiento pepper	50 mL
1	dry shallot, peeled and chopped	1
1 tbsp	chopped fresh parsley	15 mL
	lemon juice to taste	
	few drops of Worcestershire sauce	
	salt and pepper	

1 Peel eggs and chop. Place in bowl and add mustard and mayonnaise. Mix well.

2 Add remaining ingredients and mix until well combined. Season.

3 Serve on a variety of toasted bread and crackers.

Belgian Endives with Gorgonzola Cheese
(4 to 6 servings)

6 oz	Gorgonzola cheese, crumbled	175 g
3 oz	soft cream cheese	90 g
¼ cup	pine nuts, toasted and crushed	50 mL
	few drops of Tabasco sauce	
	freshly ground pepper	
	Belgian endive leaves	

1 Place both cheeses, pine nuts and all seasonings in food processor. Blend until creamy and well incorporated.

2 Spread small amount of mixture on Belgian endive leaves and arrange on platter. Serve with cocktails.

Smoked Salmon on Pumpernickel
(4 to 6 servings)

3 tbsp	butter	45 mL
1 tsp	horseradish	5 mL
6 oz	smoked salmon	175 g
	thin slices of pumpernickel bread	
	caviar (optional)	
	extra virgin olive oil	
	freshly ground pepper	
	thin slices of lemon zest	

1 Mix butter with horseradish. Spread over slices of bread cut into squares. Arrange salmon in single layer on bread.

2 Sprinkle with caviar. Add few drops of oil and season with pepper. Garnish with lemon zest.

All-Purpose Cheese Spread
(6 to 12 servings)

½ lb	soft cream cheese	225 g
3 tbsp	softened butter	45 mL
2	dry shallots, peeled and chopped	2
2 tbsp	capers, chopped	30 mL
3	anchovy fillets, drained and finely chopped	3
	freshly ground pepper	
	pinch of paprika	

1 Place all ingredients in bowl. Mix together until creamy and well blended.

2 Spread on toasted rounds of bread, assorted crackers or serve with crudités such as celery sticks and cucumbers.

Basic White Sauce

(yield: 1¾ cups (450 mL))

3 tbsp	butter	45 mL
3 tbsp	all-purpose flour	45 mL
2 cups	milk, heated	500 mL
	salt and white pepper	
	pinch of ground cloves	
	ground nutmeg to taste	

1 Heat butter in saucepan over medium heat. Sprinkle in flour and mix very well. Cook 1 minute over low heat.

2 Add milk, 1 cup (250 mL) at a time, whisking between additions. Add all seasonings and mix again.

3 Cook sauce 12 minutes over low heat, stirring often during cooking.

4 Use immediately or cover with plastic wrap, touching surface. Sauce will keep up to 2 days in refrigerator.

Note: For **Extra Thick White Sauce**, use 1½ cups (375 mL) milk instead of 2 cups (500 mL)

Homemade Garlic Butter

(yield: ½ lb (225 g))

½ lb	softened unsalted butter	225 g
2	dry shallots, peeled and finely chopped	2
3	garlic cloves, peeled, crushed and chopped	3
1 tbsp	chopped fresh parsley	15 mL
	freshly ground pepper	
	lemon juice to taste	

1 Place all ingredients in large bowl. Using wooden spoon, mix together until well blended.

2 Mound butter on large sheet of doubled foil. Form butter into cylindrical shape and roll up in foil. Twist ends shut.

3 Chill in refrigerator until firm or freeze for later use.

4 To use, simply unroll foil and slice off desired amount of garlic butter. Wrap tightly again and store.

Egg Dressing
(8 to 10 servings)

4	hard boiled eggs, mashed	4
2	egg yolks	2
1 tbsp	Dijon mustard	15 mL
1 tbsp	chopped fresh parsley	15 mL
1	shallot, peeled and chopped	1
1 tbsp	chopped pimiento pepper	15 mL
2 tbsp	lemon juice	30 mL
⅓ cup	olive oil	75 mL
	salt and freshly ground pepper	

1 Place mashed eggs, egg yolks and mustard in bowl. Mix well.

2 Add parsley, shallot, pimiento pepper and lemon juice. Mix again.

3 Incorporate oil gradually, whisking constantly. Season well and chill until ready to use.

Barbecue Sauce for Brochettes
(6 to 8 servings)

2 tbsp	olive oil	30 mL
3	dry shallots, peeled and chopped	3
3	garlic cloves, peeled, crushed and chopped	3
½	jalapeño pepper, seeded and finely chopped	½
6	tomatoes, peeled, seeded and chopped	6
½ tsp	thyme	2 mL
1 tsp	oregano	5 mL
1 tbsp	basil	15 mL
1	bay leaf, crushed	1
	salt and freshly ground pepper	

1 Heat oil in sauté pan over medium heat. Add shallots and garlic; cook 2 minutes over low heat.

2 Add remaining ingredients and mix well. Cook 18 minutes over low heat, stirring occasionally.

3 Serve with brochettes.

INDEX